I'M NOT

WHO I

THOUGHT I WAS

I'M NOT

WHO I

THOUGHT I WAS

CHRISTINE CAINE

GEBER

I Am Not Who I Thought I Was

Geber Publishing
PO Box 1252
Castle Hill NSW 1765

First published 2001, reprint 2002
Copyright © Christine Caine 2001

ISBN 0 9578719 0 2

Printed by JS McMIllain Printers
Cover artwork by Russell Hampson, photography by Fem Shirtliff, hair by Lena and makeup by Wendy Peters

Bible references come from the Amplified Bible or New King James Bible unless indicated.

* some names have been changed

dedication

To My darling Nick- My gift from Heaven

Mum & Dad – I could never thank you enough

Pastors Brian & Bobbie Houston – For your love,
support and incredible vision

To Jesus Christ, Healer of my soul –
Thank you for loving me to wholeness

IT IS NEVER TOO LATE TO

BE WHO YOU MIGHT

HAVE BEEN

George Eliot

contents

foreword

Each one of us is a rare and unique individual with a God-given destiny to fulfil. We each have a unique call that only we can carry out. We must take the necessary steps to let go of what lies behind and take hold of what lies ahead before we can discover what our true purpose in life is.

The fact is that most of us have experienced some type of abuse, rejection, or hardship in our past. Although we cannot erase it, we can overcome it through a relationship with Jesus Christ. Second Corinthians 5:17 says, "**If any person is [ingrafted] in Christ (the Messiah) he is a new creation (a new creature altogether); the old…has passed away. Behold, the fresh and new has come!**"

I believe that the foundation for finding freedom and fulfilling our destiny is in understanding who we are in Christ.

This knowledge is obtained through the continual study of God's Word. Jesus said, **"If you abide in My word [hold fast to My teachings and live in accordance with them], you are truly my disciples. And you will know the Truth, and the Truth will set you free."** (John 8:31,32)

I have learned that true freedom comes from living what the Word of God says instead of focusing on the disappointments and pain of our past.

The facts about our past are powerless against the blood of Jesus and the Truth of His Word. What Satan meant for evil, God desires to use for our good and the good of others. I believe as we allow our thinking to be renewed by God's Word and cooperate with the leading of the Holy Spirit, we will begin to inherit His promised land for our lives.

Christine Caine is an awesome woman of God who loves the Lord and desires to see people set free from the bondage of their past. In *I Am Not Who I Thought I Was,* she shares her testimony of hope and the process of her healing. It is clear, practical, and easy to understand. It will challenge you to ask yourself some serious questions, and give you helpful steps on how to overcome the obstacles of your past. It will also help you take hold of the predestined purpose for your life, enabling you to experience the sweet satisfaction of walking in the perfect will of God.

Joyce Meyer

Joyce Meyer Ministries

Christine Caine

Introduction

O f all the principles on earth, Truth is the most powerful. It has the capacity to separate our past from our future and reality from perception. When Christine's life powerfully encountered truth, she was dramatically changed. Her past ceased to dominate her present - no longer did it have the power to shape her future. Christine chose to embrace truth with all her heart and soul. She allowed it to transform her world, and a magnificent young woman has emerged.

As you read this book and step into her world, you will discover someone who could have remained contained, but instead chose to be free. You'll encounter someone who could have stayed a victim, but instead chose to be a victor.

A key to her victory came as she allowed herself to be planted in the House of God. Here she encountered God's unrestrained love.

Sadly, too many lives are marred by experiences similar to that of Christine. God yearns to reach each life with His perfect rescue plan. Allow this story to stir your heart.

I love this girl and count it a blessing from above that she is in our world.

Bobbie Houston
Senior Pastor, Hillsong Church

author's note

I t is my heartfelt desire to see all people set free from the bondages and limitations of the past and to be able to confidently embrace their future.

I believe if we discover our true origin and eternal purpose in life, which is found in Jesus Christ, we will come to realize that we are not who we think we are - **we are so much more.**

Every human being on the planet is unique and created by God in His image. Often obstacles, hurdles, challenges and pain come across our path and end up violating this original image. Subsequently, our divine nature is left bruised, destroyed or hidden: wrapped in the cloak of life's circumstances and experiences. We display this outer garment to the world, while internally we are a mixture of broken fragments that God is longing to restore to His original image.

I have tried to communicate this first part of my journey with transparency and authenticity.

This story reflects my experience and I acknowledge that not everyone responds to crisis as I have. My desire in sharing some of the intimate details of my life with you is to show that the Word of God transforms us through the renewal of our minds. The Word can do in a moment what could otherwise take years.

At the time of writing, the news of my adoption is only 20 months young, and I am still on the journey of processing the full implications of it.

Some may think I am putting pen to paper too soon, but this story is not about my adoption. Rather, I hope my past will help to give others a future.

I want to pay tribute to all those whose lives have helped to shape my thinking, especially my Pastors, Brian and Bobbie Houston, Joyce Meyer and Casey and Wendy Treat. Your teaching is so ingrained into the fabric of my being that at times, I am sure your words have flown from my heart onto the page. Thank you for helping me discover that I AM NOT WHO I THOUGHT I WAS.

Christine Caine

chapter 1

The Journey [BEGINS]

It was sobering to find out **I WAS NOT WHO I THOUGHT I WAS**. As I phoned my relatives and friends to tell them the 'family secret' was out, I found most of them already knew. I felt so exposed and vulnerable. That day, every fact I thought to be true about my conception, birth, parents and family history, turned out to be a lie.

It was one week before my thirty-third birthday. I had just finished an appointment and had 10 minutes to swallow some lunch before the next one. As I sat down to have the first bite of my favorite beef vindaloo, my mobile phone rang. I seriously wanted to ignore it, but being a woman of the 21st Century I had to answer the call.

I was greeted by a very distraught sister-in-law

who, having made sure I could talk, thrust the phone into the hands of my 35 year old brother George. He was highly emotional and sobbed as he told me he had just received a letter from the Department of Community Services (DOCS) notifying him of the fact that he had been adopted at birth.

My Mum had taken George's seven year old daughter to school. George and his wife had forgotten something at Mum's place and had gone to pick it up. As they pulled into the empty driveway they intercepted the postman. If it had been five minutes later or any other day, he would never have been at Mum's place and never received the letter.

Thinking this was all a huge mistake, I proceeded to make jokes about how this explained why we were so different. I told him to phone them and tell them there had been a massive error in their administration process.

About 10 minutes later, George phoned me back and this time he was hysterical.

"Christine, it's true. They told me my biological mother was a 15 year old girl who had become pregnant by her boyfriend. They told me where I went to school, when I was immunized and when I got married. They have my entire life on file!"

Reality suddenly hit me (and I never did get to eat my vindaloo!) All I could think of was that Mum, who had evidently kept this secret for years, was about to walk unknowingly into a very volatile situation.

I begged my brother not to say anything to her until I got to her house. I phoned and arranged for my husband Nick to meet us there.

As I was driving (very fast) to Mum's house, I phoned my best friend Kylie to tell her the news. I had a knot in my stomach as I recalled a conversation I had with Dr Lois Burkett, a minister from the USA, one month earlier.

We were in a café in Sydney's eastern suburbs having a great meal when Dr Burkett looked across the table and said, *"Christine, how is your relationship with your mother?"*

I have learnt that when Dr Burkett asks a question, there is always something deeper that she is getting at. Having been in this situation with her before, I began to consider all the recent conversations I had with Mum.

I simply answered, *"Fine, as far as I am aware."* She paused and then said, *"I have been praying for you recently, and each time I do, I cannot locate a matrix."*

I looked at her, unsure of the meaning of

matrix, *"That is a great name for a movie!"*

She smiled, *"A matrix, Christine, is a womb, a place of origin, and each time I pray for you I cannot locate this."* She paused and let the words settle.

I immediately recalled a prayer counseling session from four years earlier. I had gone to see a counselor because I had experienced abuse at an early age (not by any of my immediate family). No one knew about it, and I felt powerless in it.

I began to share with Dr Burkett about a profound moment I had experienced during this counseling session.

I felt totally disconnected from my mother. In fact, the entry in my prayer journal on that date says, "I am not supposed to be here (in my mother's womb), there is no umbilical cord, I am not connected."

After leaving the café, I decided to meditate daily on Psalm 139 and reflect on every reference to the word matrix in the Bible. Then came my brother's unexpected phone call.

As I got closer to my Mum's house, Kylie asked, *"Christine, what if you find out you're adopted too? Maybe that's what all this matrix stuff is about."* Neither of us really believed it.

My Mum had arrived home moments before me. I ran into the house, only to find my brother handing her the letter. My Mum's gasp was enough to confirm my worst fear. George really was adopted!

I stepped into the 'mediator role' as emotions started to flare. Eventually tempers settled and we all sat around the kitchen table.

Mum started to cry as she told us there was no biological reason why she could not conceive, but after several years of trying to get pregnant, she and my Dad decided to adopt.

From the outset, they had made the decision to never tell us as they always considered George their own. They could not have imagined that adoption laws could change so dramatically in 35 years.

After telling us this story and shedding many tears, my Mum looked across the kitchen table at me. My heart skipped a beat. Somehow I knew what she was about to say.

It was as if God, in His amazing love, had been preparing me for this moment for the past month. I felt His tangible presence and peace literally surround me.

After our eyes had been locked for a few seconds she said, "Christine, since we are telling *the truth, do you want to know the whole truth?"*

I stared back at her across the table, the same table we had shared thousands of meals at, had countless conversations with friends and family and celebrated many a birthday and anniversary, and the realization hit.

"I've been adopted too."

With tears streaming down her face, she just nodded. I sat in stunned silence, and finally blurted,

"Am I still Greek?"

This was one of those dream-like moments. My eyes panned the room, first to my brother; completely devastated, then to his wife in total shock; and then to my Mum; who appeared to vacillate between the relief that the secret had finally been revealed, and the fear that her children would never forgive her.

Nick came and hugged me. I was numb and at a complete loss for words. I had a moment to catch my breath as George and Mum held each other. It felt surreal as I wondered what else in my life was a lie.

We began to talk about the whole truth. My younger brother Andrew was the only biological child.

I asked Mum how she could have allowed me

to believe that the many trips I had taken to trace my roots in Greece, were authentic? How did she feel each time I had asked her why my hair was straight and every other family members wavy, or why I was so short and everyone else almost six foot tall?

I realized why, when preparing for her 60th birthday party, we only found one picture of her pregnant in the hundreds we searched.

We talked about the time when I was eight years old and Mum was making traditional Greek Easter biscuits. As we looked on, eating most of the dough, she asked us what we would do if we ever found out we were adopted. I remember answering that I would not care, as I could never have asked for better parents. I vividly recall this conversation because Mum was so obviously moved.

As we talked about the last 35 years, Mum admitted, though this was causing us pain, that she was relieved that it was finally out in the open.

We sat and talked for another hour, and then there was really nothing left to say. We each needed to go and process this 'bombshell' in our own way.

I hugged Mum tightly, assured her of my love and gratitude and then left.

I turned on my mobile phone and I immediately received a call from Pastor Bobbie. We chatted and I casually said, *"Guess what I just found out? I have been adopted."* She laughed (what else could you say at that moment? It was all too much to take). She asked if I was all right then lovingly ministered to me in a way only a spiritual mum could.

God graciously had been preparing me for this news for a month, and then ensured I would be surrounded by love from the moment I found out.

God is so personal, and desires to be a part of each moment of our lives. He showed me through this experience that He was holding me in the palm of His hand. He gave me the precious gift of friends to walk me through this phase of my journey.

THE POWER OF GOD'S WORD

My friends and I talked for hours that night. Some asked me if I was angry, others wondered how one begins to process such staggering news.

Apart from the fact that I knew God was with me before, in the midst of, and after the event, I also found that the Word of God which was stored in my heart had cushioned me in my crisis.

All of the years of reading the Bible, listening to countless sermons, and following Christ, were building a secure foundation for this very moment.

I was able to find comfort in the fact that God's Word revealed the Truth concerning my conception and life plan.

"For You did form my inward parts: You did knit me together in my mother's womb. I will confess and praise You for You are fearful and wonderful and for the awful wonder of my birth! Wonderful are Your works and that my inner self knows right well. My frame was not hidden from You when I was being formed in secret [and] intricately and curiously wrought [as if embroidered with various colors] in the depths of the earth [a region of darkness and mystery]. Your eyes saw my unformed substance, and in Your book all the days [of my life] were written before ever they took shape, when as yet there was none of them." *(Psalm 139:13-16)*

God was there from the moment of my conception. In fact, before I was ever conceived, I existed in eternity. I can be confident in my future because of Jesus Christ. I may not be who I thought I was, **but I am who He says I am**.

THE POWER OF CHOICE

I had a choice to make that day: I could allow the news of my adoption to destroy my life, or I could allow the Truth of the Word of God to build my life.

"I call heaven and earth to witness this day against you that I have set before you life and death, blessings and the curses; therefore choose life that you and your descendants may live." (Deuteronomy 30:19)

On finding out about my adoption, I had to allow the reality and life of God's Word to protect me against the natural emotions of rejection, hurt and abandonment. I cannot deny the reality of these emotions, but I did not have to let them rule my life and potentially destroy my destiny.

THE POWER OF PURPOSE

Although I was shocked to find out I was adopted, God knew all along. This news did not alter God's blueprint for my life. We are designed by God for accomplishment, engineered for success and endowed with the seeds of greatness.

The Apostle Paul put it this way:

"For we are God's [own] handiwork (His

workmanship), recreated in Christ Jesus, [born anew] that we may do those good works which God predestined (planned beforehand) for us [taking paths which He prepared ahead of time] that we should walk in them [living the good life which He prearranged and made ready for us to live]" (Ephesians 2:10)

The plan that God has for our lives usually complements the gifts and personality that He has placed in us. His desire is that we use our gifts for His glory, to build His kingdom, thus finding fulfillment and completeness.

The sad truth is many people never discover there is a divine design for their life.

I was powerfully reminded of this reality after speaking at a youth conference in Victoria, Australia. I had just finished telling my story when a young girl named Rachel* came to talk to me.

"Excuse me Chris, do you have a few minutes?" I turned to see a very nervous 19 year old standing behind me waiting to be invited to sit down. My heart melted, as I could see the deep pain in her eyes. We started to talk about life, boys, dreams, boys, the camp, and you guessed it, boys.

I quickly established that Rachel was not a Christian and that her mother 'forced' her to come to the conference. She had lived a wild life for someone so young, and the scars of rejection, bitterness, hurt and loneliness were already evident.

After almost an hour, Rachel stated, *"I had an abortion two weeks ago, and my boyfriend has left me."* We talked for a while longer and I realized that her main concern was not that she had aborted a child, but rather, that she no longer had a boyfriend.

"Rachel do you think you did anything wrong when you had the abortion?" I asked. She looked at me like I was an alien and replied, *"Of course not Christine. What else could I have done? After all, I really want to travel."*

At the core of those chilling words lie a worldview that essentially devalues human life and reduces us to little more than a cosmic accident at best, and an inconvenience to a comfortable lifestyle at worst. There is no sense of a divine purpose or plan for our lives, and we become little more than a commodity to be used or discarded at will.

I remember sitting through numerous science classes at school where the teachers tried to convince us that in the beginning there was nothing. Then nothing collided with nothing and something was formed: the cockroach. It had a genetic mutation and subsequently, the frog evolved. After a while the frog genetically mutated and there evolved an ape. The ape was walking around the planet one hot summer's day and went to the hairdresser, had a cut, shave and blow dry, and here we are today. (Admittedly none of the teachers put it quite like that, but that is how my overactive imagination interpreted this bizarre theory).

In its various forms, the theory of evolution has caused people to believe the fundamental lie that we came from nothing, we live for no apparent reason, and we are going nowhere after we cease to exist on earth.

This worldview is destructive because if we take purpose and hope away from human beings we will end up with a world full of selfishness, greed, crime, violence, injustice and pain - a world much like the one we live in.

If we tell a generation long enough there is no ultimate purpose for their life, invariably they will begin to live like they have no future.

Many express amazement at the choices young people make in relation to drugs, alcohol, suicide or transient relationships, but these are often a reaction to a deeper angst in their soul. Human beings have a need for intimacy, meaning, significance, security and a future hope.

There are so many people trying to numb their reality because they do not know there is a greater purpose for their life on earth, or that their temporal circumstances can be changed.

The logical by-product of believing the theory of evolution (or at least being profoundly influenced by it) is that the temporal becomes our measure of reality. Therefore, the gratification of our own senses is of foremost importance. We want to feel good right now. We end up substituting sex for love, casual relationships for commitment and material possessions for true identity.

People make decisions based on what they perceive will maximize their own happiness without any real understanding of the eternal consequences of their choices.

Initially, I was amazed that Rachel could be so casual about her abortion in light of the fact that she had just heard my story. I then realized she was part of a generation which had been raised without moral absolutes, or a concept of ultimate truth.

Rachel was able to feel sorry for me, and was moved by my story, but had managed to keep it totally disconnected from her own life. It had not occurred to her that the decision she made two weeks earlier had affected anyone other than herself.

If my own biological mother had made the same choice, I would not have been talking with Rachel that afternoon.

Rachel's choice is a product of a society that attempts to function without God. She made a decision based on what she considered to be the best outcome for her future. Unfortunately, the fundamental belief she held about life and death was wrong.

I told Rachel I was glad that even though my biological mother chose not to keep me, she had at least waited to have me before she went 'traveling'. Rachel sat in stunned silence for a long time. I think this was the first time she understood the magnitude of the consequences of her choice. Sitting before her was living proof of what could have been.

Christine Caine

chapter 2

The Journey [FULLY ETERNAL]

It was the Thursday afternoon before the Anzac Day public holiday. I was at work when I saw my next-door neighbor and her son running through the store, obviously looking for me. My heart immediately skipped five beats.

My Dad had been battling lung cancer for eight months. During that time, he went from being a strong, healthy man, to a 50kg (112 lbs.) skeleton because of the treatment. He had lost all of his hair and could not walk without the aid of a cane. He had been continually in and out of hospital, and my Mum had lovingly cared for and nursed him throughout the entire ordeal.

I cannot even begin to imagine the anguish and pain my Mum experienced as she held our family together in the midst of endless tests, treatments, remissions and relapses. She worked every day, looked after us kids and nursed my father.

I had been living in denial, basically relegating his sickness to little more than a bad case of the flu. I was sure he would get over it. I loved my Dad and could not bear to think that there was even a possibility that I would lose him. I hated the very thought of death.

For the first time in months, we had planned a holiday celebration as the doctors had told us that Dad was in remission. I wanted to finish work so I could spend time with my family, most importantly, Dad.

I hesitated before I stepped into my manager's office and took a deep breath. Margaret looked at me and with a trembling voice whispered, "*Christine, I'm so sorry, it's all over, your Dad has died.*" A deafening silence which seemed to last for hours followed, as this news lingered in the air.

"*No!! It can't be true!!*" I yelled. "*The doctors said he is in remission. We are all celebrating this weekend,*" my voice trailed off.

In the midst of my tears and denial, Margaret embraced me.

Mum was helping Dad put on his shirt before

going to the oncology ward for a final check up. My Dad began coughing and literally had a stroke, falling back dead in my Mum's arms. They were home alone. She screamed for help and tried to resuscitate him. Somehow she called an ambulance. Terrified and helpless, she waited out the longest 10 minutes of her life.

As the ambulance screamed out of the hospital driveway, turning past the local high school en route to our place, my younger brother Andrew and three of his friends were driving out on their way home. As soon as Andrew heard the sirens, a chilling fear hit him, He instantly broke out in a sweat as they followed the ambulance.

The ambulance officers tried to revive Dad for 30 minutes but he was gone.

Meanwhile, I was at work unaware that friends and family had already begun to congregate at our house to offer their support. At some point, amidst the grief, someone realized that I did not know that Dad had died, and Margaret had volunteered to break the news.

To this day I do not know quite how I made it home. I stopped outside my house to find an ambulance in the driveway and the front yard full of people.

Reality, grief and guilt overwhelmed me at

that moment. Why didn't I do more? Why wasn't I more supportive? Why didn't I believe that this sickness was real?

People stood in shock and the whispers began. "He was such a good man, a great husband and father. Why did he have to die when there are so many evil people in the world?" "He was so young, life just isn't fair." "What will happen to Catherine and the kids?"

I walked in the front door. At 19 years of age, I was confronted by the first corpse I had ever seen – that of my Father. I knelt beside Dad with tears streaming down my face asking the one question that no person could answer - WHY?

As I stared at him I wondered where his mind, will, intellect and emotions had gone. I could still smell his familiar aftershave. I could taste the salt of his sweat as I kissed his cheek and I felt the softness of his still warm body. Yet, undoubtedly something was missing. He was not there.

I remember thinking I had been told that there was life if you could see, taste, touch and smell it. I could do all of these things but something was evidently missing. It was my Dad's spirit.

A feeling I had experienced subconsciously time and again suddenly flooded me. A sense that God had abandoned me, like I had done something wrong but I was unsure what. That dark scream deep inside of me, which desperately needed to come out, was again repressed. I had to be strong for everyone else.

There were times in my life I had wondered why someone had not saved me from the pain and heartache. Wasn't I worth saving? I wondered why my Dad had gone through all of this, only to die. Wasn't he worth saving?

My Dad was such an amazing man. He adopted two children and gave us so much love. He took us to school, to sporting games, celebrated our lives with us.

Together with Mum, he took an unnamed two-week-old girl into his home and gave her a name. Not just any name, but Christine – 'follower of Christ'. How prophetic that proved to be.

It could not have been for nothing. Surely this was part of a bigger picture, a greater plan, some kind of eternal purpose. To limit it all to a brief temporal existence made no sense. To try and live with that explanation would be unbearable.

My Dad's death altered my life forever. There was no doubt in my heart that there was more to life. There had to be a greater reason for our lives than just being born by 'accident', living without purpose, and dying without hope.

There had to be another context in which to place this life - **something like eternity.**

ETERNITY

During the 1940's in Sydney, Australia, an alcoholic named Arthur Stace was living a life without purpose or meaning until He experienced a radical conversion to Christianity.

He was illiterate but wanted to let people know that it was Jesus Christ who had given him a new start in life and a great future. He learnt to write the word 'eternity' and spent the next decade prolifically writing this subtle reminder on footpaths and buildings across Sydney. He used this simple, yet powerful, evangelistic tool to help get people future-focused.

He became so famous throughout Australia, that his 'eternity' has become a recognized trademark.

So radical was the impact of this one word, that at Sydney's millennium celebrations, it was 'eternity' that illuminated the arch of the Sydney Harbour Bridge.

Eternity is such a profoundly powerful word and I am unsure if the organizing committee realized the significance of this word being televised live around the globe.

Eternity is God's idea. God is an eternal being, and time, as we know it, is only an insertion into eternity. In fact, the Bible says that God has placed eternity in our hearts.

"He has made everything beautiful in its time. He also has planted eternity in men's hearts and minds [a divinely implanted sense of a purpose working through the ages which nothing under the sun but God alone can satisfy], yet so that men cannot find out what God has done from the beginning to the end." (Ecclesiastes 3:11)

At the dawn of a new millennium, a proclamation went out tothe world declaring that in each and every human being, there is a divinely implanted sense of a purpose, which nothing but God can satisfy.

It was this realization that hit me as I knelt by my Dad's body 14 years earlier.

THE SEARCH FOR MEANING

Deep down, people desire a purpose for living that goes beyond the temporal. In the search for that elusive 'something' we attempt to satisfy the yearning with relationships, drugs, money, sport, travel or career.

Although there is often some short-term satisfaction in these pursuits, the deepest longings of our soul still remain unfulfilled because ultimately we are all designed to be satisfied by God. The world is full of people who have EVERYTHING to live **with** but NOTHING to live **for**.

If we all had a worldview that encompassed eternity, I am convinced the planet would look very different. All of our individual, social, political, economic, environmental, scientific, medical, and legal decisions would be made from a different perspective. We would consider the eternal ramifications of our choices and not just instant solutions or immediate gratification.

I was in a bookshop in Fremantle, Western Australia when a businesswoman ran in, obviously distraught. She was desperately seeking someone to give her a tarot reading. My ears pricked up as the shop assistant told her it was 40 dollars for a 10 minute reading, 80 dollars for 20 minutes and 100 hundred dollars for 35 minutes (this is definitely a lucrative industry!) I felt sorry for this woman as she began telling anyone that happened to be listening that her lover had just walked out on her.

She was looking for something to hang on to; a sense of hope to help her believe there was still a future for her, and she was willing to pay any price to get it.

I so desperately wanted to give her God's

reading for her life (and I would have done it for free.) He says, **"I know the plans I have for you, declares the Lord, plans to prosper you and not to harm you, plans to give you hope and a future." (Jeremiah 29:11 NIV)**

I may not have known the intricate details of her past, but I was confident that God wanted to give her a great future. I watched the woman walk out of the bookshop after a 30 minute reading, her eyes still filled with hopelessness. Sadly, in her time of need she was given a cheap substitute instead of God's perfect Truth.

TRUTH AND HOPE

Truth and hope can only be found in Jesus Christ. We can search for it everywhere, but His Word is the foundation of Truth.

Jesus said, **"I am the way, the truth and the life. No one comes to the Father except through me." (John 14:6)**

In the movie *"Shirley Valentine"*, the central figure made a powerful statement at the end of her life.

"I've led such a little life and even that will be over pretty soon. I've allowed myself to lead this little life when inside me there was so much more. It's all gone unused and now it never will be. Why

do we get all this life if we don't ever use it? Why do we get all these feelings and dreams and hopes if we don't ever use them? That's where Shirley Valentine disappeared to, she got lost in all this unused life."

Just like the fictional Shirley Valentine, many of us have been lost in all of this unused life given to us through Jesus.

He came, **"that [we] may have and enjoy life, and have it in abundance [to the full, till it overflows]." (John 10:10)**

DESTINY

God has given us the capacity to dream, the desire to live and a divinely implanted sense of purpose, to enable us to fulfill our destiny.

Destiny is the 'why' of our existence, the reason each of us was put on the planet. God has a destination for everyone and He desires that each of us reach it. Ultimately, this is to know Christ, to serve Him and to live as He did on earth.

Destiny is a journey that encompasses our relationships, marriages, children, careers, finances, and other pursuits. They are all part of our eternal purpose.

The gifts, talents and personality God has given

us exist to help us in fulfilling our destiny. God designed and equipped us to do the very things He has placed us on earth to do.

We were never designed to just exist and die, but rather to have an influence in our world for the cause of Jesus Christ. He has saved us from purposeless living.

The entire Christian faith is intentional and full of purpose. We must have a revelation of this so we can begin to live the adventure of the Christian life.

Our destiny is to complete the good works that God has prepared for each of us. There will always be challenges, hurdles and obstacles on the way to fulfilling our destiny, but we must not allow these to stop us.

There are no formulas that can save us from living in a fallen world, or the consequences thereof. The key is to trust the person of Jesus Christ in the midst of life's unpredictability. Only He can give us hope, joy and peace that surpasses natural understanding.

The journey is not so much about following a plan, as it is about passionately pursuing Jesus.

In fact, we can be confident about two things in life. Firstly, in this world we will have trouble. Secondly, we can take heart as Christ has overcome the world.

"I have told you these things, so that in me you may have [perfect] peace and confidence. In the world you have tribulation and trials and distress and frustration: but be of good cheer [take courage; be confident, certain, undaunted]! For I have overcome the world. [I have deprived it of power to harm you and have conquered it for you]." (John 16:33)

Our destiny is secure because of the work of Jesus Christ on the cross. If we believe God is good and trust in Him despite the circumstances, we will fulfill our destiny.

The Truth vs. The Facts

The Truth of God's Word is always more powerful than the 'facts' of our circumstances. Our eternal destiny is always determined by the Truth of the Word of God. The facts are often contrary to the Truth.

I was confronted by this reality through my adoption and subsequent search for my biological mother.

My brother George embraced his biological family wholeheartedly from the start. His mother never wanted to give him up for adoption, but her father had forced her to. In 1960's Australia there was much shame associated with being a pregnant, unmarried, migrant woman. These young mothers were greatly encouraged to choose adoption.

As soon as the adoption laws changed, George's mother began to actively pursue contact with him. After the initial letter, my Mum was included in this process, and they quickly bonded.

I actually needed several months to get used to the idea that I had a different biological mother to my brother.

I had no overwhelming desire to contact this woman. Although she had given birth to me, she was a stranger and had played no part in my life.

I was traveling continuously during this time and had many opportunities to share about my adoption. After each meeting I ended up speaking to many people who had either been adopted or had given up a child for adoption.

I found myself lying awake at night wondering what my story was. Eventually I contacted the adoption center and filled in the forms to start the search for my biological mother. Soon after, I received my birth certificate and hospital records.

I was a little nervous as I opened the envelope

at home alone. I pulled out my original birth certificate. This was a somewhat interesting experience, given that I had been married, and obtained a passport and other official documents with what I had always thought to be my original birth certificate.

My biological mother's name was recorded on the form, however, in the box next to father's name was the word 'unknown'. Even more devastating than this was what appeared next to the box where my name should have been: 'UNNAMED'.

My heart sank. I stood in my kitchen sobbing as I held this piece of paper, feeling so alone, rejected and abandoned.

My mind was filled with many thoughts. I wondered why this woman who had carried me in her womb for nine months did not want me. Why did she not even name me? Was I conceived out of love or at a party one drunken night? Or was I the result of a rape?

As I sat crouched over and crying, God reminded me of His Word.

"The Lord has called me from the womb; from the body of my mother he has named my name." (Isaiah 49:1)

At that point I grabbed my Bible. With it in one

hand, and my birth certificate in the other, I had a choice to make. Was I going to accept the facts that appeared on my birth certificate or the Truth contained in the Word of God?

Both were 'just' ink on paper and it would take as much faith to believe one as the other. This decision would affect the course of my destiny.

I chose to throw my birth certificate to the floor and began to confess God's Word **until** I believed it. The battle for my destiny was very real at that point. The enemy would have loved to have stolen, killed or destroyed my future. My response in this tense and critical moment could have either given him the victory, (he could only have what I gave him) or allowed Jesus to outwork through my life what He died to give me – victory peace, love, joy and strength. I chose to follow God's Word in the midst of the challenge and gave His word priority in my life.

As Christians, we need to take a victorious approach to the challenges of life because Jesus has conquered the world. This is the essence of the Christian faith. The redemptive work done on the Cross has given us the power to choose to be free from painful and binding emotions and attitudes.

Unresolved issues in our lives only serve to

make us less effective in fulfilling our destiny. Not only are our lives affected in that we do not experience the abundant life we are called to live, but we also impact all those we are supposed to influence on the other side of our obedience. The pain of obedience is always better than the pain of defeat or regret. Our position is one of liberty and we need to pursue it.

HE CALLED US OUT TO TAKE US IN

Some people do not fulfill their destiny because they could never get past the fact that they were adopted, or abused, or raped, or divorced, or rejected, or declared bankrupt, or hurt by a church or pastor, or told they were stupid and would never amount to anything.

We must remember that God called us out of Egypt (bondage, slavery and a prisoner mentality) to TAKE US INTO the promised land (freedom, liberty, victory, abundance). His plan was never for us to keep doing laps around Mt. Sinai (the same obstacles and hurdles in life) lost in the wilderness.

The one purpose for God bringing us out of our past and bondage is to take us into the awesome future He has for our lives.

"Then He brought us out from there that He might bring us in, to give us the land of which He swore to our fathers." (Deuteronomy 6:23)

What should be an 11 day journey to wholeness (metaphorically speaking) takes us 40 years because we lose focus along the way. We end up wasting much of our life going around the same mountains, just like the children of Israel.

"It is eleven days journey from Horeb by the way of Mount Seir to Kadesh Barnea. Now it came to pass in the fortieth year, in the eleventh month on the first day of the month, that Moses spoke to the children of Israel according to all that the Lord had given him as commandments to them." (Deuteronomy 1:2-3)

God does not want us to deny the pain of our past or to be totally absorbed by it. His desire is that we grow through our problems and not get bogged down by them.

God wants us to press on toward the promised land and not be consumed by the obstacles and hurdles of life. Pursuing Jesus must be our highest priority.

The territory out of Egypt, away from our past is often unfamiliar. Some of us fear this unknown terrain because we have become accustomed to living in the desert of our problems. We need to get equipped to embrace and conquer life beyond our past.

This Christian walk is a fight. It is a battle to lay hold of the eternal plan Christ Jesus has for us. We must focus our attention and energy on fighting the battles that are concerned with eternal issues rather than temporal ones, always remembering:

"For we are not wrestling with flesh and blood [contending only with physical opponents], but against the despotisms, against the powers, against [the master spirits who are] the world rulers of this present darkness, against the spirit forces of wickedness in the heavenly (supernatural) sphere. Therefore put on God's complete armor, that you may be able to resist and stand your ground on the evil day [of danger], and having done all [the crisis demands], to stand [firmly in your place]." (Ephesians 6:12-13)

If we maintain an eternal perspective of life, we live this adventure understanding that there is a fight, but we have the victory in Christ.

The Word of God is our offensive and potent weapon against the darts of the enemy. To become skilled victorious warriors in whatever we are called to do in life, we must know and appropriate God's Word in every circumstance.

"For the Word that God speaks is alive and full of power [making it active, operative, energizing, and effective]; it is sharper than any two-edged sword, penetrating to the dividing line of the breath of life (soul) and [the immortal] spirit, and the joints and marrow [of the deepest parts of our nature], exposing and sifting and analyzing and judging the very thoughts and purposes of the heart." (Hebrews 4:12)

Our role is to bear witness to the Truth in all aspects of our life. Jesus said:

"For this cause I was born, and for this cause I have come into the world that I should bear witness to the truth." (John 18:37)

Our ability to respond to the pressures and challenges of life by applying God's Truth is the litmus test to the world. If they see that the Word works they will believe it to be true.

chapter 3

The Journey [A SOUL ADVENTURE]

Nick and I were having a beautiful dinner and talking about all of the exciting things that lay ahead for us. This was a rare night where we had no other meetings to attend or deadlines to meet, and we could exclusively enjoy each others company. He took my hand in his across the table and looked deeply into my eyes and said, *"Honey, do you know what my greatest goal in life is?"*

I was waiting for a romantic monologue expressing his complete love, but instead he said: "One day, I want to be able to love you almost as much as you do!"

I was momentarily stunned and then began to laugh hysterically. I responded, *"Oh well babe, it's in your best interest that I love myself this much."*

He looked at me in amazement and asked the logical question, *"Why?"*

I replied, *"What is the greatest commandment in the Bible?"*

He cautiously answered, *"To love the Lord our God with all our heart, mind and strength."*

"Well finish it off - it does not end there," I said.

"And to love your neighbor AS YOU LOVE YOURSELF."

"That is exactly right! And that is the heart of the problem with most of humanity. We do love our neighbor just as we love ourselves, it is just that we do not really like ourselves," I said.

There was a brief moment of silence as we thought about the implications of our conversation. We realized how much God had restored my soul for Nick to be able to make that comment – it was a huge compliment.

I had spent all of my teenage years and early 20's totally imprisoned in my mind with feelings of fear, guilt, and shame because of the abuse. I really did not like myself at all, let alone have the ability to love myself.

There is a powerful prayer in 3 John 2:2 that confirms how important a healthy soul is to God.

"Beloved, I pray that you may prosper in all things and be in health, just as your soul prospers."

The soul is our mind, will, intellect and emotions. These are the tools with which we build our future. Sadly, many people are using blunt or broken tools and are left wondering why they are unable to fulfill their purpose.

There are people who are successful in their career, have amassed much wealth, or are highly educated, but cannot keep their marriages together or are addicted to artificial substances or similar. They may appear to have it together on the outside, but they have a sick soul on the inside.

We are living in a time when almost 15 per cent of the population is in some type of psychotherapy. Bookshops have entire shelves dedicated to topics such as 'how to heal your soul', or 'caring for your soul'. People are looking for answers as they bear the scars and pain of past abuse, rejection, divorce, poverty and abandonment.

We often carry wounds from our past into our lives, families, workplaces, relationships or ministries. Regardless of how well we learn to hide them, they will inevitably be revealed. They often manifest themselves as fear, insecurity, compulsive behaviors, eating disorders, anger or immorality.

AUTO PILOT - LEARNED RESPONSES

We tend to react to circumstances according to learned responses from our past. Often this hinders us from moving into our future.

I was in Nashville, USA staying with Nancy Alcorn, the founder of Mercy Ministries. I wanted to go to lunch but Nancy was in a meeting. Instead of making me wait, she threw me her car keys and suggested I take our friend Sarah with me. I was very excited, as I had never driven in America (little did Sarah realize that she was about to be my 'guinea pig').

In Australia, we drive on the left hand side of the road, and the steering wheel, gear stick and rear vision mirrors are to the left of the driver. In America, cars are designed back to front. I almost broke my hand each time I went to change gears and instead bashed the door. Each time I tried to indicate, I turned on the windscreen wipers, and I kept looking up to the roof in search of the rear vision mirror.

We finally arrived at our destination. Sarah was almost white with fear, as I am sure were some of the Americans driving alongside me! I drove that vehicle in the same way I had always driven.

I had held a license for 15 years and I had

developed countless automatic responses. I could change gears without thinking about it, look into my rear vision mirror without a conscious thought, and it was second nature to drive on the left hand side of the road.

I did not realize how many of my driving patterns were learned responses until I was put in a different environment. I then had to work very hard to develop a new driving routine. I felt like a novice all over again.

In life, just like in the car that day, we have to unlearn old habits (often with a few mistakes along the way) in order to fulfill our God given purpose on earth. We have to retrain ourselves to respond to life and its challenges from a Biblical perspective.

For most of us God's way is not the natural way of doing things. Often we have spent years reacting out of our emotions, rather than responding from the Truth of His Word.

RESTORATION BEGINS

There was a period of time in my mid-20s when God began to pinpoint areas of my soul that had been wounded or broken, with the intention of bringing healing and restoration (He continuously does this, but this was a particular time of accelerated growth and an 'intense' period of Holy Ghost 'surgery').

I came to accept I needed help, as I kept coming up against the same barriers of rejection, fear and guilt whenever I wanted to go to the next level in God. I did not like myself, or my behavior, and prayed that God would change me.

Some of my reactions to things and interactions with people were coming out of a hurting soul, and if not addressed, I would not have had an emotional foundation strong enough to fulfill my destiny.

As I began Christian counseling, I found that I had developed many defense mechanisms in my life to cope with some of the pain, and to try to protect my heart from ever being hurt again. Joyce Meyer says, "hurting people, hurt people." I discovered that I had been reacting to people and circumstances out of my own pain.

I had filled my life with activity, which was largely fuelled by a desire to somehow get rid of my past. I was always writing, working, reading, studying or on my way to somewhere else. I would rarely stop and enjoy the moment. I now know that 'keeping busy' was a cover for avoiding painful flashbacks to my past.

THE SYMPTOMS

I had an overwhelming and unhealthy need to be in control of everything in my life, even though I could not see it at the time. I wanted to create a safe environment where I could never be powerless or hurt again. Rather than trusting God with my heart, life and future, I tried to take it into my own hands.

This greatly affected my relationships. I really had no idea what appropriate boundaries were, or how to build healthy God- centered friendships. I would repeatedly find myself in emotionally co-dependant relationships that were damaging.

The fact that I did not trust God for my safety and security was at the heart of these relationships. I demanded from people what only God could give.

I also had a great fear of being rejected. I have come to understand that this was undoubtedly linked to the moment of my conception, but for many years I had no idea why I needed acceptance so desperately.

In order to get the significance and security I was searching for, I became a perfectionist and extremely performance driven.

I finished high school having won major academic, sporting and service awards. I felt valued and worthwhile only if I was achieving. This was a very dangerous foundation on which to build my self worth.

I kept placing unrealistic expectations on myself, and eventually something had to snap. I was a pressure cooker waiting to blow.

I could not even say the word abuse in reference to myself. I did not want to believe that it really happened to me, and perhaps it was all really in my head. I tried to cover all of the guilt and shame that was buried deep inside me. The guilt that somehow I had asked for it, I deserved it.

For this reason I did not like to draw any attention to my body. I had put on a lot of weight, cut my hair short and did not wear makeup.

I wanted to ensure that I never looked like I was asking for it again.

My public image was really a reflection of what was happening on the inside.

I used to say that God was not concerned with external appearances but only with the internal state of our heart. I also believed that those who took care of their physical appearance were carnal and shallow.

This was until God set up a divine appointment one Wednesday afternoon in the local sandwich shop. I had gone in to buy my mandatory chips (fries) and scallops topped with tomato sauce (ketchup) and vinegar (the ultimate 'carb' fix). There at the counter stood a very thin, (waif-like actually) blonde woman ordering a salad sandwich on wholemeal – "hold the butter please." I was perplexed at how someone could make it through the day with so little sustenance!

I actually had recognized Kylie from church and we began to chat briefly. This was to prove the beginning of a friendship that God used powerfully to help restore me.

I was passionate about working with young people (and my chips and scallops) while her passion was the gym. We were opposite in every conceivable way.

We made a deal; I would go to the gym if Kylie agreed to volunteer at the youth center I managed.

I thought I was doing my God duty by helping her become more spiritual, while all along, God was using Kylie to rebuild my shattered self-image.

Life- Divinely Orchestrated

I would never have thought someone like Kylie could have helped me, and that a salad sandwich could lead to what remains a pivotal friendship in my life. I could have just as easily missed it.

God divinely orchestrates relationships and circumstances to unlock the chambers of our heart. Once unlocked, the healing and restoration can take place.

It had taken a long time to shatter my soul, and it would take time to heal it. Friendships like Kylie's, and a strong church family helped me to walk through the valleys and not give up. We were never designed to do it alone.

It took hours of prayer and counseling over many months for God to do the deep work of unraveling the past to bring healing to my life. Regardless of how gifted or talented I was, I would always remain broken and vulnerable, unless I submitted myself to the healing process. It was vital I stayed committed to counseling, going to church, and being a part of an accountability group.

In order for these things to be effective, they had to be accompanied by a fundamental change in my thinking. Behavior modification was not my ultimate desire; I needed a heart transformation. It was the work of the Holy Spirit in my life that brought this to pass. I had to be willing to allow the 'hard soil' of my heart to be 'plowed' in order to receive the seed of the Spirit.

I had to admit that my way of thinking was so far removed from God's way of thinking. I had to accept the need for change, and then be prepared to do whatever it took to get my breakthrough.

I have found the process has been aided by the constant application of the following principles.

1. I CHOOSE TO RENEW MY MIND

"And do not be conformed to this world, but be transformed by the renewing of your mind, that you may prove what is that good and acceptable and perfect will of God." (Romans 12:2)

This verse does not exhort us to be transformed by the **removal** of our minds, but by the **renewing** of our minds. Our minds are the control center of our lives, and our hearts, the engine room.

Ultimately, it does not matter how our minds

have been programmed in the past, we can change our future by re-programming them according to the Word of God. It is only through the power of the Truth of His Word that we can discover ultimate healing and liberty. God is able to 're-oil' the engine room of our heart and bring change; if we allow Him.

When I first became a Christian some of my family and friends were worried that I would be 'brainwashed'. I certainly have been. My mind was filled with years of lies, fear and negativity. It desperately needed cleaning. I still need daily 'brain washing' according to the Truth of God's Word.

I had to undertake a commitment to the daily renewal of my mind. I did not know how to think God's thoughts, nor did I understand His ways. I began what has become a lifetime pattern of retraining myself to think according to God's Word and not my circumstances or my past.

We need to honestly assess what the greatest influences on our thinking are. Is it the media, education, politicians, economists, music, parents, friends or tradition? In order to experience transformation in our lives, God's Word must take precedence over these.

It is not God's will that our thought processes,

responses, and actions are the same as the pattern of the world. We are called to be different.

The word 'transformed' in the Greek means metamorphosis. This brings about change in the substance of a thing. Just as a caterpillar enters a cocoon and becomes a butterfly, God desires us to immerse ourselves in His Word and experience a change in our very nature.

Renewing our mind by daily meditating on God's Word ensures that our very substance is changed. **The foundation upon which our thinking is formulated is the key to our healing and destiny.**

It took me years to believe the Truth contained in God's Word and to live in the victory of God's covenant promises. I had allowed myself to live according to who I thought I was. It is liberating to live according to who God says I am.

2. I CHOOSE TO LEAVE MY PAST BEHIND

"Brethren I do not count myself to have apprehended; but one thing I do, forgetting those things which are behind and reaching forward to those things which are ahead, I press toward the goal for the prize of the upward call of God in Christ Jesus." *(Philippians 3:13-14)*

It was a major breakthrough in my life when I finally was able to admit that I had been abused. I was able to understand why I made certain choices in my life and why I repeatedly responded to things in certain ways.

God wanted to bring healing, wholeness and function to my heart (I wanted this too), but I was scared of going back to go forwards. I had spent many years covering up, denying or ignoring the reality of my past, and I could not fathom why I had to go through the pain of digging it up again. Yet, I was unable to move forward until I chose to deal with and leave behind the mess that was my past.

It is vital that we understand the blood that Jesus shed on the Cross does not give us amnesia. I have often heard people use the phrase, 'it's under the blood' as a way of ignoring or denying their past. Our past did happen, and the hope that we have in Christ is a life beyond our past. He does not want us to ignore our past, but to grow through it into our future.

I had really struggled with allowing God into the deep recesses of my heart. I realized that I did not truly trust Him. Even when I consciously began to let God in, it was still a gradual process. God is so gracious, loving and patient, that He gently and slowly began to show me His goodness. He allowed the circumstances of my life to be used as opportunities to prove His personal and intimate love. He brought people into my life at pivotal times to help guide me and help me to trust again.

As I began to change, I understood that I had gained a part of my identity from my brokenness and pain.

It was a real challenge to let go of that identity and to accept my new identity in Christ. This identity was a whole, restored and redeemed Christine. With this new identity came a responsibility to walk out a life of wholeness. Deep down I feared that I could not.

Often I was so paralyzed by this fear of failure, I would not make any progress for months at a time. Fear of failure only cripples us into inaction.

Allowing the past to dictate our future ultimately thwarts God's purposes and plans for our life. So often we can allow the labels of our past (stereotypes, our upbringing, words spoken over us or socio-economics) or past injustices (an ex-pastor, the church, ex-spouse, abuser) as an excuse for not living in victory.

We often live as though there is a special disclaimer clause for our particular situation or circumstance.

The truth is, the Bible contains no disclaimer clause. Christians have been set free from the bondages of their past through the blood of Christ.

"Yet in all these things we are more than conquerors through Him who loved us." (Romans 8:37)

Ultimately, I had to choose to keep pressing through and eventually let go of the past and the identity that I had taken on, so I could lay a hold of the future.

3. I Choose To Forgive Those That Have Hurt Me

"For if you forgive men their trespasses, your heavenly Father will also forgive you. But if you do not forgive men their trespasses, neither will your Father forgive your trespasses." (Matthew 6:14-15)

I had finally come to the place where I really wanted to move beyond my past and I was ready to forgive those who had hurt me. I was receiving help from a married couple, and as we were praying through the past pain and rejection, the husband said, "Christine now it is your turn, you have to forgive them."

I remember sobbing and sobbing as I knelt for hours unable to articulate the words, "I forgive". When I finally didsay them, I experienced a deep sense of release that had been waiting to come forth for 20 years.

I could not have moved forward in my Christian walk if I did not come to this place of total brokenness and reliance on God. Only He could give me the capacity to forgive them.

It is not an issue of whether they deserved forgiveness. It all comes back to Jesus. He forgave me for the debt I owed Him, therefore I have no choice but to forgive others for the debt that they owe me.

Forgiveness is incredibly powerful and liberating - spiritually, physically and emotionally. This power is truly a miracle of God - we cannot do it alone.

The only way I could ultimately sever ties with my past and embrace the future was by forgiving those who had hurt me.

The one thing worse than being abused, would be to carry the perpetrators of that abuse with me in my heart forever through unforgiveness.

The power of forgiveness has set me free.

4. I Choose To Take Every Thought Captive To Christ

"[Inasamuch as we] refute arguments and theories and reasonings and every proud and lofty thing that sets itself up against the [true] knowledge of God; and we lead every thought and purpose away captive into the obedience of Christ (the Messiah, the Anointed One)."
(2 Corinthians 10:5)

It was a real discipline to train my mind to reject thoughts that were not of God and to replace my thoughts with God's thoughts. I had spent many years cultivating negative thoughts and these were not going to disappear overnight.

I thought I was of no value and that God could not use me because of my past. The truth is, God considers me (and you) priceless, and wants to use me despite my past.

I went to the Bible to find out what God had to say. The Word made it clear that I could be free from the pain of my past. I was not living this, nor did I really believe it. I thought anger, insecurity and fear would always be a part of who I was.

I had to replace my thoughts with God's thoughts by confessing His thoughts daily (For me, this was the most time-consuming and difficult part of the process.) There were many times that I would have preferred to remain in my own self-justified negativity. It took energy and exertion to bring my mind in line with God's Word.

In order to be truly free, I had to make the Word my reality. Eventually, God's thoughts became my thoughts and I began to walk in the fullness of His promises.

As I began to think differently, my thoughts produced a brand new way of living. **When it comes to building our destiny, we move in the direction of our thoughts.** God's thoughts lead to life and hope. As His thoughts became my thoughts, I began to possess the future He had for me.

It was after a sustained period of ongoing commitment to the basics that the changes became evident.

I started to think, speak and respond differently. I had a definite hope about my future and the gifts God had given me to fulfill my purpose. I was no longer fearful or trying to please people from a wrong motivation.

I no longer kept busy to avoid flashbacks, I lost weight, began to dress differently and began to walk in a new found confidence. I believed I was created in the image of God and His desire was that I be fruitful in every area of my life. I no longer had to live a contained life. I was free in my mind and heart to pursue my destiny.

5. I Choose To Obey God

"Jesus answered If a person [really] loves Me, He will keep my word [obey My teaching]; and My Father will love him, and We will come to him and make Our home [abode, special dwelling place] with him." (John 14:23)

Simple obedience did not come naturally to me, but until I could prove obedient in my current circumstances and environment, I could not move to the next level in God.

God was working on my character. He wanted me to learn love, patience, kindness, longsuffering and self-control. He allowed me to be confronted by circumstances that helped develop these qualities in me.

There were many times that nothing in my flesh wanted to do the right thing, but the only way forward was obedience. There were certain places that I could not visit, movies I could not watch, conversations I could not have and friends I could not keep.

I also made a decision to continue to be active in all aspects of church life, regardless of my feelings.

It came down to a simple choice: **my will or God's will?**

As I began to discover the awesome benefits of pursuing God, it became easier to resist my fleshly desires. Obedience was not so much about giving up something good, but rather chasing something better. I wanted intimacy with Christ, and there was no cost too great for this privilege.

To experience Jesus in our lives, we must demonstrate our love by obeying Him.

chapter 4

The Journey [A HIGHER PURPOSE]

We had been planning our holiday for months. Kylie, Sally-Anne and myself were ready for a well-earned break. Kylie had organized a cruise to take us up the east coast of Australia, as far as Cairns, Queensland. We had then planned to take a scenic drive from Cairns to Port Douglas before flying home on Sunday afternoon, in time for church Sunday night.

We waved our families goodbye as we sailed out of Sydney Harbour for 10 days of rest and relaxation. The cruise was beautiful. We did little more than read and soak up the sun.

All too soon, the ship had docked in Cairns and it was time to disembark. We intended to hire a sports car in the morning and then set off on what is reputably one of the best drives in Australia.

As we were walking to our hotel, Bruce*, a guy we had met on the cruise, (he also happened to live in a neighboring suburb in Sydney), came up to us and asked what our plans were for the following day.

After explaining Bruce told us he and his friend were planning to hire a four-wheel drive and do the same thing. He suggested we pool resources and do the drive as a group.

I thought this would be a perfect opportunity for us to share the Gospel, and since there was three of us and two of them, it would be OK.

The girls and I checked into our hotel, excited about the prospect of going four-wheel driving for the first time.

I did not really believe Bruce and his friend would be awake at 6am to pick us up, but I was wrong. At 5.50am I heard a car horn. We quickly grabbed our swimming gear, cameras and bags and ran to the front of the hotel to be greeted by what looked like an oversized toy truck. I grabbed a tourist map from the hotel counter and we set off.

Bruce drove the first leg of the journey and the scenery was even more beautiful than I could have imagined. We stopped for breakfast and decided to take the coastal route up to Port Douglas and back to Cairns through the Daintree Village.

It took a few hours to get there, and being the Girl Scout I am (not!) I figured that three hours was two finger spaces on the map, and the trip home was three finger spaces. According to my calculations, it would take a third of that distance again to get back to our hotel (do you wonder why no-one has asked me to lead any major expeditions lately?)

We headed towards the Creb Tree Track, which cuts through the Daintree Rainforest. As I reached down for the map, I realized it was no longer there. Undaunted by the mere loss of a map, we decided to press on and find our way back based on instinct.

We were having such an awesome adventure that we lost all sense of direction and time.

I have since learned that this track is one of the top four-wheel driving routes in Australia, and best reserved for experienced drivers. The track is off limits during the wet season and up to three months following.

Due to some recent deaths, the track had been closed, but all notification signs had been removed. We had no idea we were entering dangerous territory!

The track was extremely slippery and Bruce was having difficulty steering. We were not going to let bad traction stand in the way of good fun, so we urged him to keep driving. As we came down another hill, the vehicle stalled in the middle of a huge mud swamp. The others began to panic, but I thought this would be an ideal opportunity to share the Gospel.

As I opened the door to assess the situation, I said, *"Look guys, don't worry I'm a Christian and God will get us out of this mess."* I momentarily gasped as I stepped into waist deep mud. *"This is a greater opportunity than I anticipated for God to prove Himself, but nevertheless He will get us out."*

I walked around the vehicle and stood behind the back tire, urging Bruce to accelerate as I tried to push us out. It was the best mudpack I have ever had! I was literally covered from head to toe.

After about two hours, I conceded we were bogged (don't forget these were crocodile infested waters and I am a café latte, inner city sort of girl).

The guys suggested we stay with the vehicle as it was getting late and we were obviously in the middle of nowhere.

My personality does not lend itself to 'just sitting and waiting', so I made an executive decision to start walking. My rationale was simply this; if on the map it was only three fingers back to Cairns, surely we had driven at least two and three quarter fingers. The Village then, had to be within walking distance.

We began to climb up what I thought was a small hill. I soon discovered this was one of the steepest mountains in the range.

I kept speaking words of life and faith the entire time but nobody was really in the mood to listen.

As night fell, light drizzle turned into heavy rain and we no longer could see the track in front of us.

I thought every noise I heard was a boat, plane or truck coming to rescue us. It is amazing what you believe when you are desperate to get out of your mess. These noises proved to be little more than the wind in the trees.

We came to the bottom of the mountain, only to face a river. There was nowhere to go but across. Bruce knew that we had a 'slight' aversion to crocodiles, and we were likely to become hysterical if we stopped to think about the situation. We had a light with five minutes battery remaining, and only after leading us into the river, did he turn it on.

Up until that moment, I was oblivious to the magnitude of the danger, or the reality of our situation. I felt hopeless. All I could see around me were mountains and trees.

After we had come so far, fatigue and dehydration forced us to stop. The plan was to continue walking at daybreak.

It was still raining in the morning. As Bruce was the only one with any energy left, he decided to walk ahead to try and find help. As the day progressed, we attempted to stay positive. As afternoon came, there was still no sign of Bruce and we realized our plane had left for Sydney without us.

Being Greek and very theatrical, I decided to make a deathbed out of leaves. As I assumed the 'death posture' (an Egyptian Mummy position) I prepared to meet my Maker. Then Sally-Anne said, *"Chris, do you hear that sound?"* Convinced she was in the final stages of delirium, I thought it was nice of God to take her home thinking she was going on a helicopter ride. After a few moments, I believed I could hear it too. Sure it was the end for me, I repented of everything I could think of and a whole lot more, just to be sure.

As I looked up, I could see Bruce overhead. I was so excited that I am sure I broke the horizontal to vertical speed record. I ran to the edge of the cliff screaming at the top of my lungs, "WE'RE SAVED."

At that instant, I realized the words that had come out of my mouth. I understood why God had allowed me to experience the ordeal of being lost in the Daintree. I felt the Holy Spirit challenge me, "Christine, when was the last time you remembered what it was to be totally lost? When did you last feel the anguish of hopelessness?"

OUR MANDATE

While four-wheel driving, I got so caught up in the adventure, I forgot the purpose of the trip, and ended up lost in the process.

Similarly, on the Christian journey, we can forget the purpose of our salvation, and end up wandering aimlessly, overcome by the obstacles and challenges of life.

I believe we should enjoy the adventure, not forgetting the mission God has given us. He has given us this mission statement:

"Go therefore and make disciples of all the nations, baptizing them in the name of the Father, and of the Son, and of the Holy Spirit, teaching them to observe all things that I have

commanded you; and lo, I am with you always, even to the end of the age." (Matthew 28:19-20)

As Christians, our mandate is to restore a broken humanity to their Creator, leading them out of darkness into light.

"You are the light of the world. A city that is set on a hill cannot be hidden. Nor do they light a lamp and put it under a basket, but on a lampstand, and it gives light to all who are in the house. Let your light so shine before men, that they may see your good works and glorify your Father in heaven." (Matthew 5:14-16)

This scripture highlights the fact that we are called to be light to the world. To be this light, we must first allow God to do His work **in us**, so as He can complete His work on earth **through us**. The very purpose of light is to bring illumination. As we receive more of God's Word, our light becomes brighter, enabling us to lead more people out of darkness.

My restoration is only the first level of God's redemption plan for my life. The higher purpose is to "go and make disciples."

Jesus said:*"Heal the sick, cleanse the lepers, raise the dead, cast out demons. Freely you have received, freely give." (Matthew 10:8)*

I have discovered you cannot give what you

have not received. While I myself was lost in the Daintree, I could not help others. Similarly, if we remain broken, we can only give out of our brokenness.

The Gospel is all about the world. In fact, God so loved the world (not just an individual) He sent His only Son to save it.

The Gospel is 'good news', and it is up to us to tell it to a lost and broken world. God has entrusted His Church with this message of hope. If we do not proclaim it, who will?

Regardless of how healed we are when we enter heaven, it is the extent to which we fulfill our mandate on earth that has eternal consequence.

My Dad's death is a constant reminder to me of the urgency of this mandate. I remember the pain and heartache I felt at my Dad's funeral. Cancer had totally destroyed his body. There would have been no cost too great to save him.

Imagine, as they were lowering the coffin, if my friend John, a doctor, had whispered to me:

"Christine, you know how my mother was cured of cancer last year? Well, I discovered that cure in my final year of medical school. I wanted to tell you about it but I was so busy attending

my medical functions, enjoying spending time with my med school friends, and so consumed with further research, I never found the time to tell you about the cure. In fact, Christine, that is not entirely true. Once or twice I actually went to the lab and took the cure out of refrigeration, but as I held it, I was so nervous about it not working for your Dad, that I put it back."

I would have been devastated if my friend had the cure for cancer and had not told me about it while my Dad was dying of the disease.

We would expect to see a discovery such as this headlined in the media worldwide. The entire planet would soon be made aware of such great news.

As Christians, we have the cure for sin - the ailment plaguing humanity. This cure is Jesus Christ.

"Since all have sinned and are falling short of the honor and glory which God bestows and receives." (Romans 3:23)

"For the wages which sin pays is death, but the [bountiful] free gift of God is eternal life through [in union with] Jesus Christ our Lord." (Romans 6:23)

At times, we allow fear or insecurity to prevent us from sharing this cure. Yet the good news of

Christ is the hope of the world.

"For I am not ashamed of the gospel of the Christ, for it is the power of God to salvation for everyone who believes, for the Jew first and also for the Greek." (Romans 1:16)

We have a message to declare, and a world that is literally dying to hear it.

OBSTACLES ALONG THE JOURNEY

To survive the Daintree, we had to trudge through a mud swamp, trek over a mountain, cross a crocodile infested river and, what proved more difficult than all of these, overcome the battle of the mind. Without persevering, we may never have gotten out.

Not all of us will experience being lost in bushland, or being abused or adopted, but we may face obstacles in our lives that can disrupt our journey.

The only way they can prevent us from fulfilling God's plan is if we stop pursuing Christ as our ultimate goal. Following Him will help us through the struggles, setbacks and confusion. If we think the goal in life is to escape pain and problems, then we will inevitably be disappointed.

In order to fulfill my God given purpose, there

were several additional obstacles I had to overcome. Although the details may differ, I have found many people struggle with similar challenges.

OBSTACLE NUMBER 1:   TRADITION

I realized how important ethnicity was to me; the day I found out I was adopted. My first question to Mum was, "Am I still Greek?"

I was brought up in a culture where a jar of olive oil was considered a low fat diet, and a light snack was a four-course meal. At family functions, we would break plates, while others ate off them. Immediate family included anyone up to a third cousin and everything we did was loud.

Within the confines of the Greek community, it was good being Greek. It was outside of this that prejudice became obvious.

At school, the other kids would laugh at me because they had vegemite sandwiches, and I had olives, fetta cheese and taramosalata. I was embarrassed because my last name, Caryofyllis, was the longest in the school. As they got to my name, I knew it would take them 10 minutes to try to pronounce it.

I remember trying desperately to do everything I could to fit in and be accepted.

This was difficult, as I was never allowed to go to parties or sleepovers because Greek girls 'did not do that sort of thing'. Instead, I grew up learning to cook the best Greek meals (my husband probably wishes I would prove to him that this is true), to dance, and speak Greek.

I grew up in pre-multicultural Australia, where the ultimate insult was to be called a 'wog'. I was made to feel second-rate and was often told to go back to 'my own country'. The only problem being, Australia was my country.

I imagine everyone in my world thought I would follow the traditional path for a Greek woman - marry young, have children and set up house. It would have been the easy and acceptable thing to do, but this was not the path God had prepared for me.

In order to fulfill God's plan for my life, I had to choose to place His Word above my culture.

God did not require that I totally discard all elements of being Greek, only those things which were contrary to His Word.

Breaking ties with the only tradition I had known was difficult, but essential if I was to embrace my destiny.

Obstacle Number 2:   RELIGION

To be Greek is to be Orthodox, and my early years were spent fulfilling the Sunday ritual of enduring Church. The liturgy was two hours long (in ancient Greek which nobody spoke). I used to love the smell of the incense (until it choked me when the priest would stick it in my face). The candles burned brightly and I was captivated by the pictures of the saints on the walls, wondering what I would need to do to get my picture up there.

Soon bored by all the ritual, I decided if this was what God was all about I would believe in Him but not really live for Him. I had enough fear of hell to plan on living for Him once I was so old that I already had one foot in the grave.

I never knew anyone actually read the Bible, or for that matter opened it. I thought it was the big gold book that people kissed as a good luck charm when they were desperate.

I could not fathom how Christianity could be relevant to anyone's daily life. I had not understood the difference between religious tradition and an authentic relationship with a living Savior. Once I experienced this relationship with Jesus, my perspective on God and Church was revolutionized.

I did not know my choice to become serious about my relationship with Jesus would cause such a huge reaction from my community. They felt I had totally shamed them for leaving the church I was raised in, and believed I had joined a 'cult'.

It was a very lonely and difficult road during this time - I had lost my entire support system. I had to learn to gain my identity from Jesus. He too had been rejected by His culture and religious tradition. If He could make it, then I knew I could.

Had I remained in this religious setting, I would never have realized God's purpose for my life. It is therefore essential to be planted in a healthy, biblically based church, only then can we flourish.

Obstacle Number 3:   GENDER

"Christina, stop playing soccer (European football) with the boys and come inside and help me with the dolmades. How many times do I have to tell you that girls do not play soccer? Boys don't like rough girls Christina, and for you to get married the boys need to see you in the kitchen."

I must have heard these words, or similar, literally thousands of times.

Mum would take me to K-Mart to buy a new doll, instead I could be found in the aisles playing with toy cars. She tried to take me to ballet, but I ripped off my tutu and refused to go again. Finally we compromised. I was allowed to play netball and softball as at least these were 'girls' sports.

I ran home with my report card topping my class to be confronted by, "*You don't need brains to get married and have children Christina. No man will want you if he thinks you are smarter than him.*"

It was as if my gender was a limitation, a lid on all the hopes, dreams and gifts locked up inside of me.

When I was the first in our family to go to University, people tried to talk me out of it so I could marry Stellios*. He was my parent's dream catch. He was from a good Greek family and owned a fish and chip shop, which also sold fruit and vegetables. They said he would not want me if I were more educated than he (which proved to be true).

The words, "*Christina you do not need a degree to have babies,*" echoed in my ears as I enrolled at University.

I cannot remember a time when my gender was not cited as a limitation to fulfill the purposes of God in my life. I never thought that women could do what I am doing today.However, as I have remained obedient to God's call, I am amazed by the opportunities He has opened up for me.

Throughout history, women have been limited by gender. At times, even the church has oppressed women because of tradition. However, Jesus Christ was one of the greatest emancipators of women.

In Jesus' day women were marginalized, particularly in places of worship. They were relegated to the back of the synagogue. Luke 13:10-17 tells us of the time Jesus was teaching in the temple and He noticed a crippled woman. He called her forward, laid hands on her and she was immediately healed. Jesus effectively put her in the 'spotlight' and snubbed the social convention of the day.

The division of the sexes was instituted by culture and tradition, not by God. In Him we are two sexes but one race.

"So God created man in His own image; in the image of God He created him; male and female He created them." (Genesis 1:27)

Women were there from the beginning, and are equal to men. Together, we were created to reflect the true image of God.

In recent times, there has been an awakening

on the planet. Both men and women are seeing that it is God's will that we partner together in building His Kingdom.

I am blessed to be a part of a dynamic church where our Senior Pastor, Brian Houston, recognizes and encourages the active participation of women in all aspects of church life.

The truth is that not everyone shares this view. Even after I married, some people told me, "*Chris, you are a woman (I was well aware of this!) and you are going to have to pull back so you have time to cook and clean for Nick.*"

In order to be doing what I am today, I had to put aside everything I **assumed about** women, and discover what God **actually said** about women.

Gender is not an obstacle to fulfilling our destiny. God knew our sex when He determined our purpose. We need to have the courage to break out of the established mold and lay hold of our future.

OBSTACLE NUMBER 4: MARITAL STATUS

Turning 18 was a milestone for a Greek woman as it meant you could now be married. Whenever I visited any of my relatives they tried to marry me off to the next eligible Greek boy - only I was never very interested.

When I was 20 and still single, my uncles would urge me to hurry up and find someone or, *"all of the really good ones will be gone."* When I was single at 24, they would say, *"Christina it is OK, some boy will still have you, don't give up hope."* By the time I was 27, and still single, I could hear all of the whispers before I walked into a room, *"Here she comes, no-one bring up marriage - the poor girl has been left on the shelf, no-one wants her. It is because of her progressive ideas and her religion. If she was just normal she would be married by now."*

I laugh now as I think of those years. I was led to believe that my value and identity would only be found in my husband and in my role as a wife and mother. I have since discovered, regardless of marital status, our identity should be found in Christ.

Whether single, married, divorced or widowed, God has a purpose for us in each season of life. If we spend our life wishing we were in another season, we may miss God's perfect will for us. Rather than viewing singleness as an obstacle to fulfilling our God-given destiny, or marriage as an excuse for 'pulling back' from the purposes of God, we need to embrace these seasons as gifts from heaven, orchestrated by God in His divine plan.

OBSTACLE NUMBER 5: SOCIO-ECONOMIC BACKGROUND

As I stood waiting to enrol in University, I overheard the conversation of the girls in front of me. They were obviously friends from a private school and I was feeling intimidated by the quality of their speech. I felt alone, being the only person enrolling from my school.

After a while the girls asked where I was from. As I told them, they literally took a step back, gripped by fear. Stone-faced they asked, "Do you carry a knife or a gun?"

This was the general view about people that came from my part of Sydney. I grew up in a low socio-economic area, and my envoironment clearly shaped my worldview (It was obvious the worldview of these girls was also shaped by theirs!)

Some people blame socio-economic background for their situation in life, but this does not have to be a limitation. I had to make a conscious decision not to be contained by this stereotype or use it as an excuse for not pursuing my destiny.

In order to fulfill my call and do the things God had purposed for me, I needed to be enlarged on the inside and gain more resources than I had.

My life was transformed when I realized my past, the economic climate, government support or my employer did not determine my future prosperity. The Bible says:

"You shall remember the Lord your God, for it is He who gives you power to get wealth, that he may establish his covenant which He swore to your fathers, as it is this day." (Deuteronomy 8:18)

It is God's will to bless and prosper us, that we in turn become a blessing to others. God did not design us to have **barely enough**. His desire is that we have **more than enough**, so we can give from our abundance to reach a lost and dying world.

To attain the promises of God for my life, I had to begin living my life according to His Word, rather than my socio-economic background. I applied the Biblical principle of sowing and reaping.

The Bible states:

"Do not be deceived, God is not mocked; for whatever a man sows, that he will also reap." (Galatians 6:7)

As I began to sow at a new level, I

experienced a greater blessing and influence across all areas of my life, including my marriage, finance and ministry.

Those who have gone before us have sown seed and we are the fruit of that seed. It is God's plan that we move beyond where we started in life (our background, neighborhood and finances) toward His predestined future for us.

Although we cannot change the past, we all have the power to change the future. Choosing to sow at a new level today will directly affect what we will reap tomorrow.

The Road Map – The Word

Leaving the map of the Daintree behind was not a sensible move. I had not anticipated how much danger we would face and how useful the map could have been.

I have already explained in detail the importance of God's Word - His road map for our life. The Word gives us direction, keeps us on track and helps us negotiate life's obstacles. It also gives us comfort in our darkest hours and hope to cling to.

To attempt to navigate the journey of life without the Word of God would be a serious 'destiny hazard'.

THE VEHICLE – THE LOCAL CHURCH

Just as we needed a vehicle to get safely through the Daintree, the local church is God's vehicle through which our destiny is outworked.

I thank God for the 13 years I have been in my local church, the Hillsong Church. The fact that I have been planted in the church has significantly influenced my healing process. The Bible is clear about the importance of being planted:

"Those who are planted in the house of the Lord shall flourish in the courts of our God. They shall still bear fruit in old age; they shall be fresh and flourishing." (Psalm 92: 13-14)

Being **planted** is different to **attending** church. When planted, our roots become strong and healthy. Within this context, healing flourishes.

I have sat under the life transforming preaching of the Word of God, been a part of corporate worship and involved in cell groups. Each of these continue to help nurture and strengthen me.

The love and mercy extended to me within this community has helped restore my soul. The church has been a safe place to process feelings of fear, doubt and frustration, on the way to restoration and wholeness. People have walked alongside me, directing me to the ultimate Healer of my soul.

I have the honor of serving under Senior Pastors who have modeled victorious Christian living. Their lives bear witness to the Truth of God's Word. This has inspired me to stay on the path of restoration and trust the Word to work in my life.

From my earliest days in the church I sensed God wanted to use me to influence lives around the world. Based on where I was at emotionally, this seemed impossible. Despite this, I began to serve in any way I could.

I have found many people are chasing their destiny somewhere 'out there'. I believe if we begin to serve where we are, God will take care of the rest.

We cannot 'short circuit' the character development process that happens most effectively within the local church environment.

Our God-given destiny can be fully realized within the context of the local church. God is building His church and we should spend our lives building what He is building.

THE GUIDE – THE HOLY SPIRIT

If we had opted to take a guide with us on our Daintree trip, we would have avoided getting lost. Similarly, we should not consider negotiating the journey of life alone.

For this reason, God has given us His Holy Spirit. He is not some impersonal cosmic force, rather our intimate friend and guide. He is by our side at all times longing to be included in our life.

"But the Comforter (Counselor, Helper, Intercessor, Advocate, Strengthener, Standby), The Holy Spirit, Whom the Father will send in My name [in My place, to represent Me and act on My behalf], He will teach you all things. And He will cause you to recall (will remind you of, bring to your remembrance) everything I have told you." (John 14:26)

I have found He is with me in the midst of every circumstance. When my Mum told me I was adopted, I sensed the presence of the Holy Spirit surrounding me. The day I held my birth certificate, I felt His arms embrace and comfort me. At other pivotal moments, He has brought to my remembrance God's Word and wisdom. These have sustained, comforted and helped guide me. I could not do life without the Holy Spirit.

Many people have courageously ventured into the dark 'alleys' of their soul but have somehow lost their way to Jesus. We can become so absorbed in our search for wholeness and healing that we end up bogged.

Although recovery from the pain of our past is to be pursued and desired, it should not absorb all our energy. We can become so immersed in our own lives that we forget the awesome wonder of a life in Christ.

The purpose of the journey is Jesus. The guide, map and vehicle all point us to Him.

chapter 5

The Journey [CONTINUES]

Friday nights had become a high light of my week since I started volunteering at my local youth center. This particular night was a relatively quiet one. I was standing outside with several members of the team, when, at 2am, Jason stumbled towards us. As he came closer I could tell he was intoxicated. I soon realized he was going to be sick. As he looked at me, he vomited into the garden and then fell face first into his own vomit. The sight repulsed me, as did the stench. I thought I was going to be sick.

As the leader of the team, everyone looked to me for direction. Feeling faint I motioned to one of the girls to go and get something to help clean up the mess. She quickly returned with two rolls of toilet paper and stood staring blankly at Jason.

I was about to delegate the clean up process to another team member when I felt an unmistakable prompting from the Holy Spirit. I 'heard' Him say: "Christine, do you see how that vomit looks and smells to you?" In my heart I answered, "Yes Lord." "Well that is exactly how your sin looked to me. I stepped into your life and wiped away the sin, now get on your knees and wipe up the vomit."

Instantly I dropped to my knees and began to clean up the mess. As I did so, I sensed the Lord say: "Christine, this is what you are going to spend your life doing - wiping up the vomit of a lost and broken generation."

As I felt the vomit run down the sleeves of my new denim jacket, I was not concerned about the mess or the inconvenience, all I cared about was Jason.

It was while wiping up the vomit on the pavement that night in 1989 that I made a conscious decision to spend my life helping others find answers in Christ.

I was 22 years old and fully committed to Jesus, but I was not planted in a local church. I was still trying to reconcile what it meant to be a

Christian. I had no framework or language to explain this defining experience and I did not understand what it meant to be 'called', however, from then on, all I wanted to do was to serve Jesus (even if this meant joining a convent in order to become the next Mother Teresa).

I believe God heard the desire of my heart that night. In response, He set in motion a series of events that led me to my current church. It seemed as if one minute I had vomit dripping down my sleeves, and the next, I was on the way to fulfilling my destiny. Within 18 months of that momentous night I had enrolled in Bible College, was fully planted in church and working in the evangelistic arm of the youth ministry.

Following this, I became the Director of the Hills District Youth Service and was extensively involved in high school seminars and community-based youth work. In 1995, I left HDYS to lead an evangelistic youth movement, Youth Alive New South Wales. Through large-scale events, youth leadership training, school and university programs, multiplied thousands of young people were reached with the message of Christ.

I marveled at how God used someone like me to help young people. It was as if everything that had happened to me in my past was turned around to benefit others. The experiences that could have potentially destroyed my life were now bringing hope.

The words of Joseph to his brothers rang true for me.

"As for you, you thought evil against me, but God meant it for good, to bring about that many people should be kept alive, as they are this day." (Genesis 50:20)

In 1997, while at Youth Alive, I received a phone call from a journalist working for the music magazine, Rolling Stone. He wanted to feature our mid– year event in the August edition of the magazine. I was excited that a publication of the magnitude of Rolling Stone would take an interest in our organization.

It was a powerful night as 5000 teenagers united to worship Jesus. The journalist was surprised that young people were embracing Christianity on such a large scale.

I did not dwell on the article until the day it hit the news stands. I was unsure if it would reflect fairly on our organization or God. My apprehensions soon faded as I opened the magazine to what was a four-page colour feature. I bought every copy in the store and made my way to a 7am staff meeting.

I was yet to read the entire article, but had gleaned enough to know it was extremely positive. I stole away to read it alone and I soon came to the following paragraph:

"Caine presents a sermon not from a pulpit but the stage. She comes across as that young, groovy teacher at school who you had a bit of a crush on. She's savvy to what you got up to on the weekend. When you passed out drunk at a school dance she woke you up and WIPED UP THE VOMIT."

I audibly gasped as I read this line. Tears flowed as my mind returned to the youth center eight years earlier. I am convinced that as surely as the Holy Spirit penned the Bible through the hands of human writers, He took the hand of the journalist and had that line included for my benefit.

As I sat stunned, I again heard the voice of the Holy Spirit say: *"Christine, don't you ever forget that it never ever gets more glamorous than this. Your life was always destined to wipe up the vomit of a broken generation. It started one on one in a local youth center, and now it may be in stadiums, but there is no difference. It never gets any bigger than the individual. As long as there is still one person on the planet who does not know me, you have a job to do. As long as you are alive, the journey is not over. You must continue to wipe up vomit."*

Needless to say, I was an emotional mess and immediately renewed my commitment to 'do whatever it took' to fulfill my destiny.

Amazing things had transpired in the years between the Friday night at the youth center and that morning reading Rolling Stone. I had experienced a measure of success, but without realizing it, some of the things that were once important to me had become less important. I allowed my focus to shift slightly. Unintentionally, I fell back into being performance driven and outcome orientated, characteristics that had defined my past.

God's reminder compelled me to evaluate the condition of my heart and the direction I was heading. I was willing to make all the necessary adjustments to ensure I did not miss fulfilling my purpose.

I left the staff meeting determined to stay focused on becoming more Christ-like. I began to look for Biblical examples of people who had run their race and finished their course. I wanted to discover the principles that would help me finish strongly.

Caleb, one of the 12 sent out from amongst the Israelites to spy out Canaan, was a man who went on to fulfil his purpose because he had a different spirit to those around him.

"But my servant Caleb, because he has a different spirit in him and has followed me fully, I will bring him into the land where he went, and his descendants shall inherit it." (Numbers 14:24)

The "different spirit" relates to the character that is being formed in us. The goal is that our character should reflect Jesus.

The danger is in thinking our destiny is determined by the gifts and talents we have. We can spend our life developing these, but ultimately they can destroy us if our character cannot sustain us.

I could not accomplish my destiny as I was. I had to choose to remain Christ-centered in all I was doing and who I was becoming.

On the completion of the famous statue of David, sculptor Michelangelo said:

"All I do is carve away everything that isn't the sculpture."

The master sculptor of our life is God. If we allow Him, He will chip away the 'self' part of our nature. His purpose is not to hurt us. His objective is to 'unveil' His image in each of us.

"Then God said, 'Let Us make man in Our image according to Our likeness...'" (Genesis 1:26a)

Although I have been radically transformed, I am still on the journey of being restored to His original image. As more of me is chipped away, more of God is revealed.

With each day, I increasingly discover
I AM NOT WHO I THOUGHT I WAS.

I'M NOT WHO I THOUGHT I WAS

TO LIVE IS CHRIST

I make a vow
My life will always honor Christ
Whether I live or die
I belong to Him
He bore my sin
I owe this life to my Saving King

Hallelujah
I am not my own
You are in control
Hallelujah

For me to live is Christ
And to die is gain
No matter what
Price I pay
I choose to give this life away

Only by the cross I am saved
Only by the cross I am saved

Christine Caine

Our deepest fear is not that we are inad-
equate. Our deepest fear is that we are
powerful beyond measure. It is our light,
not our darkness, that most frightens us.
We ask ourselves, who am I to be brilliant,
gorgeous, talented and fabulous? Actually,
who are you not to be? You are a child of
God. Your playing small doesn't serve the
world. There's nothing enlightened about
shrinking so that other people won't feel
insecure around you. We were born to
make manifest the glory of God that is
within us. It's not just in some of us; it's in
everyone. And as we let our light shine, we
unconsciously give other people permission
to do the same. As we're liberated from our
fear, our presence automatically liberates
others.

Marianne Williamson

Thankyou

Joyce Meyer – For being an inspiration and role model. Your life is a great example to us all.

Bobbie Houston – you are my 'Mum' in the faith. I love and honor you beyond words.

Kylie DiMauro – If it was not for you, I would not be here. Thanks for going the distance. Lotta love from me to you always.

Dianne Wilson – I could not do this without you. Thanks for the 20 hour plane trips, encouragement and endless support.

Maria Ieroianni – You are amazing. What was life like before you? Thanks for the late nights, early mornings and constant rewrites.

Rebekah Woodward – You are the grammar queen. Thanks for the laughs.

Shanelle Hall – My soul buddy. Thank you for believing in me.

Molly Venske – You give 'Sleepless in Seattle' a whole new meaning. Thanks for the laughs, the tow trucks and the memories.

Merilyn Buckley – For being a true friend. Thanks for rearranging your life to help me. I am so grateful Heaven orchestrated our friendship.

Geoff Woodward – For the desperately needed male perspective.

Daryl-Ann Leroux – For your constant emailing and keeping me to deadline.

Jeff Crabtree, Bayliss Conelly & Kevin Brett – For the prophetic 'kickstart'.

Russell Hampson – You are a creative genius.

Lena Nimmo – I did not recognize myself

Wendy Peters – Nick did not recognize me.

Fem Shirtliff – Nobody recognized me!

Kate Spence, Jill Tooth, Deb Malcolm, Helene Enevoldson, Sarah Vassallo, Elise Mann, Renee & Kelly, Bev Spence, Belinda Thomas, Kathy & Lyn Saunders, Nicole Avila – thanks for your input and encouragement.

I'M NOT WHO I THOUGHT I WAS

Christine Caine

CHRISTINE CAINE

Christine Caine is a dynamic and passionate visionary whose powerful testimony of restoration is impacting thousands of lives around the world each year. She, her husband Nick and daughter Catherine live in Sydney, Australia and are based at Hillsong Church.

Her personal experiences and her grasp of the issues shaping the 21st century, enable her to effectively communicate a relevant message of hope.

As one of Australia's leading Christian communicators, Christine's inspiring message is impacting people of all ages across Australia, Asia, Europe, the USA and Canada.

Her vision is to help people overcome the obstacles, hurdles and challenges of life in order to fulfill their God given potential and purpose.

For more information on other available resource, go to www.chriscaine.com